The Magic Mone

In go five pennies.

Out comes a nickel!

In go five pennies and one nickel.

Out comes a dime!

In go two dimes and one nickel.

Out comes a quarter!

In go five nickels.

Out comes a quarter!

In go five dimes.

Out come two quarters!

In go two quarters.

Out comes a half-dollar!

And now . . .

In go twenty pennies, one nickel,
one quarter, and five dimes.

Out comes one dollar!

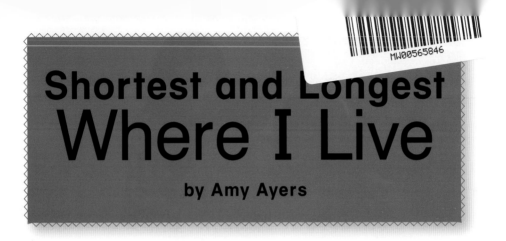

Shortest and Longest
Where I Live

by Amy Ayers

Printed in China

ISBN 13: 978-0-15-360216-0
ISBN 10: 0-15-360216-3

11 12 13 0940 16 15 14 13
4500409957

Harcourt
SCHOOL PUBLISHERS

This is our home.

My family lives here.

We have things of many lengths.

The shortest shoe is pink.

The longest letter is blue.
It is for my dad.

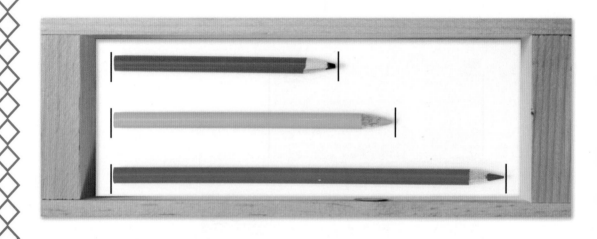

The shortest pencil is green.
It is in a box.

The longest spoon is wooden.
My mom stirs things with it.

The shortest picture is of a flower.

The red car is longest.
Red is my favorite color.

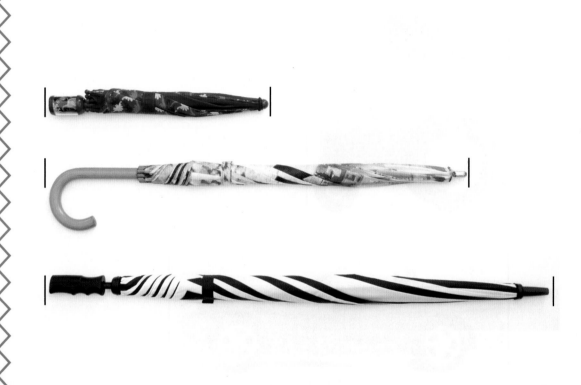

The shortest umbrella is blue.

My toothbrush is on top.
It is the shortest!

Glossary

letter

shortest

longest

spoon

pencil

toothbrush

picture

toy

shoe

umbrella